FARM ANIMALS

SHEEP

Katie Dicker

W
FRANKLIN WATTS
LONDON • SYDNEY

 An Appleseed Editions book

Franklin Watts
First published in Great Britain in 2017
by The Watts Publishing Group

© 2013 Appleseed Editions

Created by Appleseed Editions Ltd,
Well House, Friars Hill, Guestling,
East Sussex TN35 4ET

Designed by Hel James
Edited by Mary-Jane Wilkins

ISBN hardback 978 1 4451 5107 6
Dewey Classification 636.3

A CIP catalogue for this book is available from the British Library

Photo acknowledgements
l = left, r = right, t = top, b = bottom
title page Eric Isselee/Shutterstock; page 3 southmind/Shutterstock; 4, 5 Hemera/
Thinkstock; 6 Monkey Business Images/Shutterstock; 7 Jupiterimages/Thinkstock;
8 trossofoto/Shutterstock; 9 iStockphoto/Thinkstock; 10 Hermin/Shutterstock;
11 iStockphoto/Thinkstock; 12 Karel Gallas/Shutterstock; 13 marilyn barbone/
Shutterstock; 14 Eric Gevaert/Shutterstock; 15 Steve Ikeguchi/Shutterstock;
16 iStockphoto/Thinkstock; Katrina Leigh/Shutterstock; 18 Marcel Jancovic/
Shutterstock.com; 19l iStockphoto/Thinkstock, r polispoliviou/Shutterstock; 20 sharon
kingston/Shutterstock; 21t iStockphoto/Thinkstock, r Paul van den Berg/Shutterstock;
b JKlingebiel/Shutterstock; 22 background iStockphoto/Thinkstock; bierchen/
Shutterstock; 23 Alexander Gitlits/Shutterstock.com
Cover Trevor kelly/Shutterstock

Printed in China

Franklin Watts
An imprint of Hachette Children's Group
Part of The Watts Publishing Group
Carmelite House
50 Victoria Embankment
London EC4Y 0DZ

An Hachette UK Company
www.hachette.co.uk

www.franklinwatts.co.uk

Contents

My world

Baaa!

I am a sheep.
I live on a farm
with lots of
other sheep.

Here are some of my flock.

Sheep do not like
to live alone. We stick
together in large groups.

Top to toe

Our thick woolly
fleeces keep us
warm in winter.

Sheep usually have a fleece
of black, brown or white wool.

Some sheep have horns, which grow all through their life.

Our strong hoofs help us walk on steep mountains, rocky surfaces or wet ground.

Keeping cool

In summer, our fleeces are cut to keep us cool. This is called shearing.

Our wool is cleaned, coloured and spun into thread. Then it is made into clothes and carpets.

Sheep shearers use electric clippers. In the past, hand clippers were more common.

Snip!

9

Time to eat

We like to eat leaves, twigs, grass and grain.
We graze for up to ten hours a day.

Sheep have four parts to their stomach to help them digest the plants they eat.

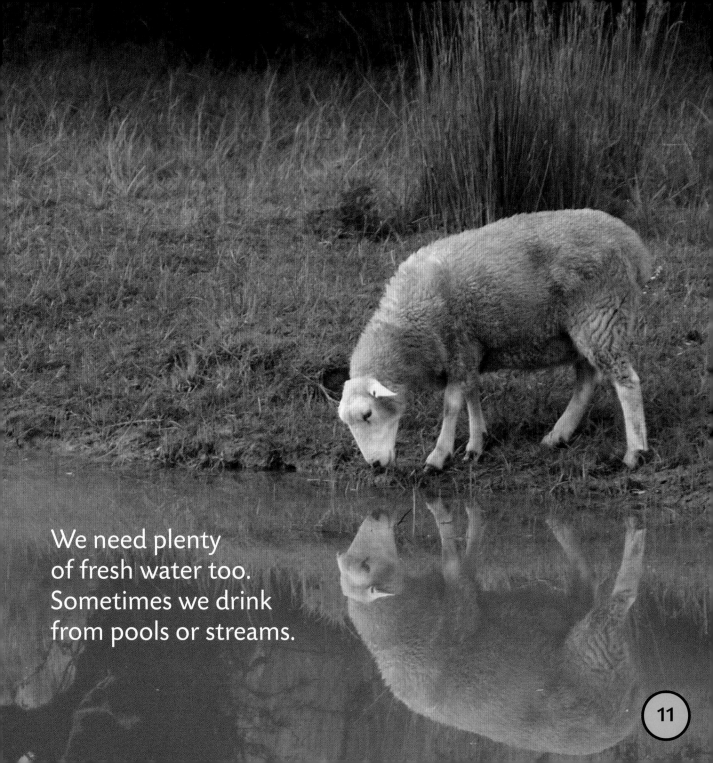

We need plenty
of fresh water too.
Sometimes we drink
from pools or streams.

Sheep and lambs

Baby sheep, called lambs, are born in spring when the weather is warm and there is lots of grass to eat.

Lambs can stand up within a few minutes of being born.

12

Young lambs drink their mother's milk. Some lambs are bottle-fed.

Lambs are born when a male sheep (a ram) breeds with a female sheep (a ewe).

Ewes often have twins or triplets. The farmer makes sure our lambs are born safely.

Sounds and smells

Lambs know the sound of their mother. They listen for their mother's call if they get lost.

Bleat!

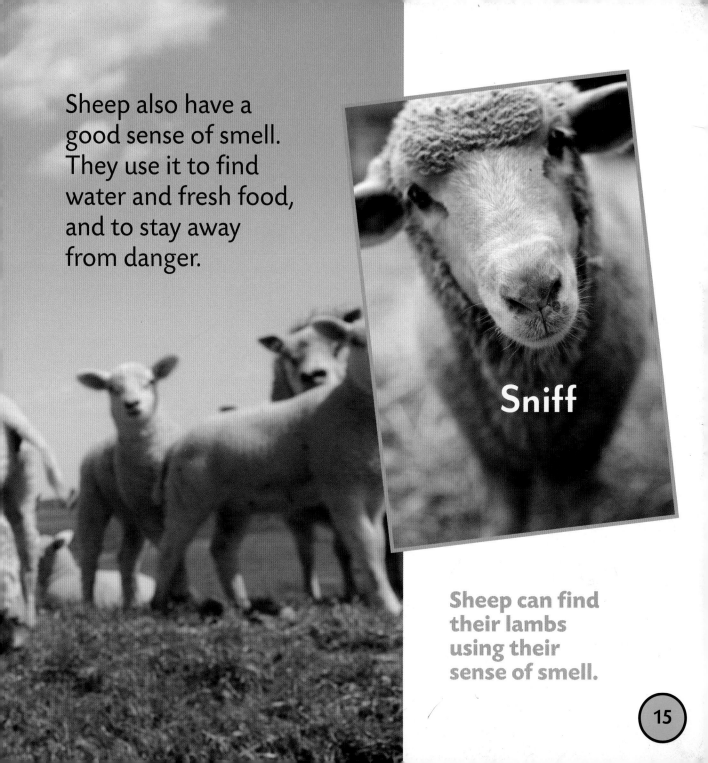

Sheep also have a good sense of smell. They use it to find water and fresh food, and to stay away from danger.

Sniff

Sheep can find their lambs using their sense of smell.

15

Who looks after us?

The farmer makes sure we have enough to eat, and helps newborn lambs to grow big and strong.

Some sheep farmers are called shepherds. They gather their sheep together to check them.

Some shepherds use a sheepdog to herd their sheep.

On large farms horses or tractors are used instead.

Farm produce

Sheep are farmed for their meat, called lamb or mutton, and for their wool and leather.

When sheep reach a healthy weight, the farmer takes them to market.

Some sheep are farmed for their milk, which can be used to make cheese and yogurt.

The milk from these Roquefort sheep is used to make cheese.

Sheep around the world

Lincoln, England

Farmers in countries all over the world keep sheep, and many sheep also live in the wild. Here are some of the different breeds.

There are more than 900 different types of sheep around the world.

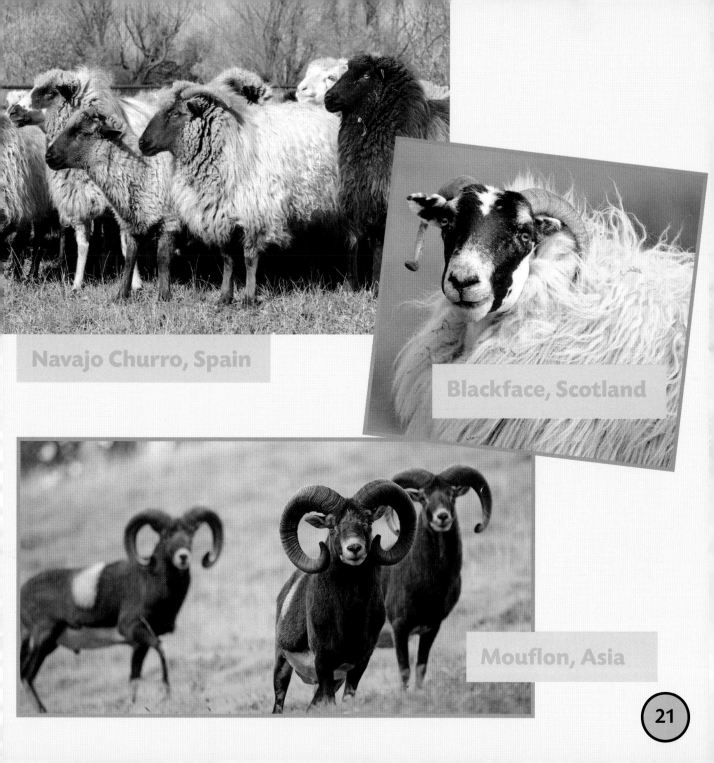

Navajo Churro, Spain

Blackface, Scotland

Mouflon, Asia

Did you know?

A sheep has no top teeth at the front of its mouth.

Sheep usually live for about seven to ten years.

A sheep grows about 3.5 kilos of wool a year – enough to make a man's suit.

An experienced sheep shearer can shear about 150 sheep a day!

Useful words

fleece
A sheep's woolly coat.

grain
A type of cereal used for animal feed.

graze
Animals graze when they eat grass.

leather
A material made from the skin of an animal.

twins and **triplets**
Two or three babies born at one time to the same mother.

Index

Websites

www.animalcorner.co.uk/farm/sheep/sheep_about.html
www.kiddyhouse.com/Farm/Sheep
www.kidcyber.com.au/tag/facts-about-sheep-for-kids/
www.kidsfarm.com/sheep.htm
www.sciencekids.co.nz/sciencefacts/animals/sheep.html